1993

Revolution and Romanticism, 1789-1834
A series of facsimile reprints chosen and introduced by
Jonathan Wordsworth
University Lecturer in Romantic Studies at Oxford

Frere
Whistlecraft 1818

John Hookham Frere

Whistlecraft
1818

Woodstock Books
Oxford and New York
1992

This edition first published 1992 by
Woodstock Books
Spelsbury House, Spelsbury, Oxford OX7 3JR
and
Woodstock Books
Wordsworth Trust America
Department of English, City College
Convent Ave and 138th St, New York, N.Y. 10031

Distributed in USA by
Publishers Distribution Center
P.O. Box C831, Rutherford, N.J. 07070

ISBN 1 85477 122 1
Reproduced by permission from a copy in
The London Library, St James's Square, London
New matter copyright © Woodstock Books 1992

British Library Cataloguing in Publication Data
A catalogue record for this book is
available from the British Library

Printed and bound in Great Britain by
Smith Settle
Otley, West Yorkshire LS21 3JP

Introduction

Known to scholars only as the source of Byron's metre in *Beppo* and *Don Juan*, Frere's *Whistlecraft* is a poem of great wit and charm, showing a writer completely relaxed and in control, talking to himself and his audience and his muse about nothing very much. It is the manner that matters. Thalia, muse of comedy and pastoral, can seldom have led so amiable and domesticated an existence. 'I've a proposal here from Mr Murray', Frere tells her at the outset of Canto III, 'He offers handsomely – the money down'. Why not a stay in the country to calm her nerves as the two of them get down to writing again:

> 'Tell me, my dear Thalia, what you think;
>   Your nerves have undergone a sudden shock;
> Your poor dear spirits have begun to sink;
>   On Banstead Downs you'd muster a new stock,
> And I'd be sure to keep away from drink,
>   And always go to bed by twelve o'clock.
> We'll travel down there in the morning stages;
> Our verses shall go down to distant ages.
>
> And here in town we'll breakfast on hot rolls,
>   And you shall have a better shawl to wear . . .
> Come, now, fling up the cinders, fetch the coals,
>   And take away the things you hung to air,
> Set out the tea-things, and bid Phoebe bring
> The kettle up.' – *Arms and the Monks I sing.*
>
> Some ten miles off, an ancient abbey stood,
>   Amidst the mountains, near a noble stream . . . (III, ii-iv)

There is a deliciousness in the juxtaposition as Frere and Thalia go down to the country by the morning stage-coach, and the poetry goes down with them – to posterity.

   No wonder Byron was delighted and inspired. The spenserian stanzas of *Childe Harold*, with their more elaborate rhyme-scheme and lagging final alexandrine, had served their purpose, but were weighty and inflexible by comparison. Here was a form that really lent itself to the speaking voice. And one, too, that had an Italian pedigree. Southey comments on the new development in a letter to Landor of February 1820:

A fashion of poetry has been imported which has had a great run, and is in a fair way of being worn out. It is of Italian growth – an adaptation of the manner of Pulci, Berni, and Ariosto in his sportive mode. Frere began it. What he produced was too good in itself, and too inoffensive to become popular; for it attacked nothing and nobody; and it had the fault of his Italian models, that the transition from what is serious to what is burlesque, was capricious. Lord Byron immediately followed . . .

Byron's interest in Frere's stanza led him in 1820 to translate the first canto of Pulci's *Morgante maggiore*, claiming on 21 February that it was 'the parent not only of *Whistlecraft*, but of all jocose Italian poetry'. So concerned was he to make his point that with infinite pains he translated Pulci line for line, insisting that the original be printed alongside. The giant, Morgante, speaks to his future master:

   'And let your name in verity be shown;
Then will I everything at your command do'
On which the other said, he was Orlando. (st.xlvii)

   'Dimmio del nome tuo la veritate,
Poi di me dispor puoi al tuo comando';
Ond' e' gli disse, com' egli era Orlando. (st.xlvii)

Confronted by a pointless, wandering story about knights and giants and monks, written allegedly by two brother harness-makers from Suffolk, Frere's first readers looked for allegory and political satire. Those who knew him to be the author were aware that he had been responsible, with Canning, for the brilliant parodies and Government propaganda of the *Anti-jacobin*. The giants must surely be the French, recently defeated at Waterloo? The wayward genius of Sir Tristram should make him easy enough to identify. And what of Sir Gawain, with his touches of Dryden's Achitophel:

Adviser-general to the whole community,
He serv'd his friend, but watch'd his opportunity. (I, xxv)

Could Gawain's inability to carry through his plans really
have no ulterior meaning:

Take his own plans, and place him in command,
   Your prospect of success became precarious:
His plans were good, but Launcelot succeeded
And realized them better far than He did. (I, xxvi)

Wellington must surely be somewhere in all this? Could
he perhaps be the 'anti-tintinnabularian' Friar John,
saviour of the monastery? But if so, what could the fable
of the bells be all about? Why should the monks want
'bells of larger size, and louder tone'? Why should bells
arouse in giants 'irrational gigantic anger'? It was, and is,
all very perplexing. And delightful.

In a learned and rambling article on *Whistlecraft*,
headed 'Narrative and Romantic Poems of the Italians',
the *Quarterly* for April 1819 refers its readers to Pulci,
Boiardo, Berni, Ariosto and Forteguerri. The writer's
quest for origins and resemblances is no great success.
More surprisingly, he is prepared to say so: 'Indeed it is
not very easy to understand the nature of the part which
the poet is acting; nor do we always know how to take
him. Sometimes he is *really* Mr Whistlecraft the harness
and collar maker'. Not often. Twenty years after his time
on the *Anti-jacobin* working (with Pitt as well as
Canning) as a bright, brittle, up-to-the-moment tory
political satirist, Frere was amusing himself. His choice of
the harness-making alias pokes fun at the fashion for
labourer poets (Ann Yearsley the Bristol Milk Woman,
Burns, Bloomfield and others), but also shows an
intention to burlesque Arthurian romance, and national
epic pretensions, from an unlettered viewpoint. The
intention seems not to have lasted very long. Far from
establishing the voice of a rural innocent, Frere found a
way, as Lamb would do in *Elia*, of being comfortably
himself under another name. As for King Arthur and his
Round Table, they scarcely got beyond the title-page.

Southey was probably right that *Whistlecraft*, 'attacking nothing and nobody', was too inoffensive to be popular, but he shows little understanding of the poetry in his objection to caprice. Whether or not it was a fault in Frere's Italian models, it is (as Byron immediately perceived) a strength in the English. There could be no 'transition from what is serious to what is burlesque' without its being made clear which is which. *Whistlecraft* has its values: concern for language, for instance,

> don't confound the language of the nation
> With long-tail'd words in *osity* and *ation* (Proem, vi)

(compare Clough's *Uranus* on 'modern ologistic fancyings'), and distrust of political process:

> it often happens in the hour of need,
> From popular ideas of utility,
> People are pitch'd upon for mere ability. (IV, xviii)

It has its beauties and exquisite observations: of the black and glossy water-skaters, for instance, as the poet and Thalia, their legs 'idly dangling down',

> Rest upon the bank, and dip [their] toes
> In the poetic current as it flows . . .
> Or mark the jetty, glossy Tribes that glance
>   Upon the water's firm unruffled breast,
> Tracing their ancient labyrinthic dance
>   In mute mysterious cadence unexpress'd . . . (III, l-lii)

But seriousness, free from caprice, *Whistlecraft* does not, and could not, have.

It is even a little difficult to be sure where there is burlesque. '*Arms and the Monks I sing*' we can all place as a take-off of Virgil ('Arma virumque cano'), but the poem as a whole hardly seems to be mock-epic. There is satire in Frere's portrayal of leadership among the knights, and faction among the monks, but it could never be said to be the point of the poetry. Swift, with the giants of Brobdingnag, makes his position clear on every page. They are crude, at times cruel, at times disgusting, but they nonetheless convict human beings of littleness.

Frere's giants exist in no such morally definable universe. They carry off ladies, roast mules and horses, eat a couple of duennas, without anyone seeming to mind. The trick, of course, is evenness of tone. Whatever takes place, the voice that tells the story insists upon a comic detachment. It may be funny, beautiful, shocking, but always (as later with Byron) it is droll:

> But first I must commemorate in Rhime
> Sir Tristram's dext'rous swordsmanship and might
> (This incident appears to me sublime),
> He struck a Giant's head off in the fight:

Tough on the giant – but what are giants for? These things are bound to happen in pursuit of the sublime. Frere has not finished with us, though:

> The head fell down of course, but for some time
> The stupid, headless trunk remain'd upright;
> For more than twenty seconds there it stood,
> But ultimately fell from loss of blood. (II, xlviii)

Nowhere does Byron offer cruelty with greater elegance. Why are we not sick? Because vivid and appalling as the scene is to the mental eye, we are still listening to the voice claiming it as comedy. The final line of the stanza (as we have come to expect) turns the scene to comic effect. Grasping with relief at a heartless (headless) joke – only the living fall from loss of blood – we read on, permitted by our sense of the grotesque to remain within the borders of unreality. It is an extreme case of Frere's control, but one among many that remind us of the only preceding English poem that shows a comparable elusiveness, intelligence, elegance, beauty of language and manipulation of poetic style, sense of proportion and power in disproportion – Marvell's *Appleton House* (c. 1650). Marvell too is writing just after a bloody war, and introduces disconcerting violence within the protected world of his poem. He too tempts us with the thought of allegory, defying us to make a definition of his mode of not quite narrative. He too controls the poetry through a voice, urbane, witty, trusted in its values, yet always at a distance.

Even some of the material of Marvell's poetry turns out to be comparable. No connection seems likely, but for a parallel to Frere's monks and their defence of the monastery, one might turn to the no less strange episode of nuns under attack in *Appleton House*. Surprisingly the one writer with whom Frere could be said to engage is Wordsworth. The ponderousness of his title page (*Prospectus and Specimen of an intended National Work . . . Intended to Comprise the Most Interesting Particulars Relating to King Arthur and his Round Table*) is surely a guying of the *Excursion*, with its Prospectus to *The recluse* and pretensions to be part of a forthcoming philosophical epic. The Wordsworth whom Frere confronts in the text, though, is at his least pompous. It is the tender, fanciful poem, *To Joanna*, that has taken his fancy, with its laughter echoing among the mountains:

> The rock, like something starting from a sleep,
> Took up the Lady's voice, and laugh'd again:
> That ancient Woman seated on Helm-crag
> Was ready with her cavern; Hammar-Scar,
> And the tall Steep of Silver-How sent forth
> A noise of laughter; southern Loughrigg heard,
> And Fairfield answer'd with a mountain-tone:
> Helvellyn far into the clear blue sky
> Carried the Lady's voice . . . (ll. 54-62)

Joanna clearly charmed her future brother-in-law. Wordsworth's lines have a gaiety unlike anything that we expect of him. Frere makes from them the high point of his poem, as first the mountain-giants, then the giant-mountains, express their disapproval at the tintinnabulation of the monks:

> Giants abominate the sound of bells,
> And soon the fierce antipathy was shown,
> The tinkling and the jingling, and the clangor,
> Rous'd their irrational gigantic anger. (III,xv)

It is extraordinary that such poetry should not be better known: the first line powerfully imaginative, the second mock-heroic in its hint of Pope ('The *strong antipathy* of good to bad'), the third vividly onomatopoeic, the fourth elegant not least in its picking up of the etymology of 'giant' (Anglo Saxon 'gigant'). Friar John, as his fellow monks scurry round setting up their belfry, has felt 'beforehand, for a fortnight near,/A kind of deafness in his fancy's ear' (III,xlv); the mountains, in 'their granite ears', are more deeply troubled:

> Meanwhile the solemn mountains that surrounded
>   The silent valley where the convent lay,
> With tintinnabular uproar were astounded,
>   When the first peal burst forth at break of day:
> Feeling their granite ears severely wounded,
>   They scarce knew what to think, or what to say;
> And (though large mountains commonly conceal
> Their sentiments, dissembling what they feel,
>
> Yet) Cader-Gibbrish from his cloudy throne
>   To high Loblommon gave an intimation
> Of this strange rumour, with an awful tone,
>   Thund'ring his deep surprise and indignation;
> The lesser hills, in language of their own,
>   Discuss'd the topic by reverberation;
> Discoursing with their echoes all day long,
> Their only conversation was 'ding-dong'.

'Those giant-mountains', Frere continues, at his most playful and enchanting,

>   inwardly were mov'd,
>   But never made an outward change of place:
> Not so the mountain-giants-(as behov'd
>   A more alert and locomotive race),
> Hearing a clatter which they disapprov'd,
>   They ran straight forward to besiege the place . . .
>   (III,xvii-xix)

Riddle: how do you tell mountain-giants from giant-mountains? Answer: they are 'A more alert and locomotive race'. Not a lot different, but they move. Frere's is an entirely delightful humour. Cader-Gibbrish (Cader-Idris) and high Loblommon (Ben Lomond) are farcical, with a touch of disrespect for Wordsworth; 'Discussed the topic by reverberation' is a line brilliant by Frere's highest standards (how many of our human colleagues do the same?); and, to crown it all, Frere in this marvellous stanza has rhymed three times – 'intimation', 'indignation', 'reverberation' – on the sound that he (or perhaps, so early in the poem, the harness-maker) expressly forbad.

Byron, first good-humouredly in *Beppo*, then with power and a much sharper cutting edge in *Dog Juan*, would possess and extend the idiom of *Whistlecraft*. But there are lasting qualities in Frere that go with his more equable temperament and benign observation of human foible. His sense of beauty and sense of disproportion are all his own. Alone among Romantic poets (Lamb the essayist is a parallel), he takes an imaginative pleasure in fancy. Who else, in the space of two stanzas, could play the fisherman, set a picnic in front of us, turn it into a still life for the collector, and, standing back, adopt the tones of the connoisseur showing off his 'cabinet jewel':

> The Monk with handy jerk, and petty baits,
>   Stands twitching out apace the perch and roach . . .
> And soon his motley meal of homely Cates
>   Is spread, the leather bottle is a-broach;
> Eggs, Bacon, Ale, a Napkin, Cheese and Knife,
> Forming a charming Picture of Still-life.
>
> *The Friar fishing* – a design for Cuyp,
>   A cabinet jewel – 'Pray remark the boot';
> And, leading from the light, that shady stripe,
>   With the dark bulrush-heads how well they suit;
> And then, that mellow tint so warm and ripe,
>   That falls upon the cassock . . . (IV,iii-iv)

J W

PROSPECTUS AND SPECIMEN

OF AN INTENDED

National Work,

BY

WILLIAM AND ROBERT WHISTLECRAFT,

OF STOW-MARKET, IN SUFFOLK, HARNESS AND COLLAR-MAKERS.

INTENDED TO COMPRISE

THE MOST INTERESTING PARTICULARS

RELATING TO

King Arthur and his Round Table.

SECOND EDITION.

LONDON:

JOHN MURRAY, ALBEMARLE-STREET.

1818.

THE following stanzas being for the most part the production of my late brother William Whistlecraft, as composed by him in the year 1813, I have judged (by the advice of my friends) that it would be more suitable to publish them without alteration in any respect, and to which I have adhered strictly, as may be seen by a reference to the thirteenth stanza. This I thought it due to have stated, in

consideration of our having proposed the
Two Boards for Verse and Prose, which in
the present crisis might be stigmatized;
but it is well known that the public opi-
nion was more consonant to magnificence
and useful encouragement at that time
than it has been for the last twelve
months, or is likely to be the case again,
unless the funds should experience a fur-
ther advance, together with an improve-
ment in the branches of Customs and
Excise. The occasion of their remaining
unpublished was in compliance with the
advice of friends, though at present, in
conformity with the pressure of the times,

they have thought it advisable that the following publication should take place, which, if an indulgent public should espouse it, it is intended that it should be followed in due course with a suitable continuation.

I.

I've often wish'd that I could write a book,
  Such as all English people might peruse;
I never should regret the pains it took,
  That's just the sort of fame that I should chuse:
To sail about the world like Captain Cook,
  I'd sling a cot up for my favourite Muse,
And we'd take verses out to Demarara,
To New South Wales, and up to Niagara.

II.

Poets consume exciseable commodities,
    They raise the nation's spirit when victorious,
They drive an export trade in whims and oddities,
    Making our commerce and revenue glorious;
As an industrious and pains-taking body 'tis
    That Poets should be reckon'd meritorious:
And therefore I submissively propose
To erect one Board for Verse and one for Prose.

III.

Princes protecting Sciences and Art
    I've often seen, in copper-plate and print;
I never saw them elsewhere, for my part,
    And therefore I conclude there's nothing in't;
But every body knows the Regent's heart;
    I trust he won't reject a well-meant hint;
Each Board to have twelve members, with a seat
To bring them in per ann. five hundred neat :—

IV.

From Princes I descend to the Nobility :

In former times all persons of high stations,
Lords, Baronets, and Persons of gentility,

Paid twenty guineas for the dedications :
This practice was attended with utility ;

The patrons liv'd to future generations,
The poets liv'd by their industrious earning,—
So men alive and dead could live by Learning.

V.

Then, twenty guineas was a little fortune ;

Now, we must starve unless the times should mend :
Our poets now-a-days are deem'd importune

If their addresses are diffusely penn'd ;
Most fashionable authors make a short one

To their own wife, or child, or private friend,
To shew their independence, I suppose ;
And that may do for Gentlemen like those.

VI.

Lastly, the common people I beseech—

    Dear People! if you think my verses clever,

Preserve with care your noble Parts of speech,

    And take it as a maxim to endeavour

To talk as your good mothers us'd to teach,

    And then these lines of mine may last for ever;

And don't confound the language of the nation

With long-tail'd words in *osity* and *ation*.

VII.

I think that Poets (whether Whig or Tory)

    (Whether they go to meeting or to church)

Should study to promote their country's glory

    With patriotic, diligent research;

That children yet unborn may learn the story,

    With grammars, dictionaries, canes, and birch:

It stands to reason—This was Homer's plan,

And we must do—like him—the best we can.

VIII.

Madoc and Marmion, and many more,

Are out in print, and most of them have sold;
Perhaps together they may make a score;

Richard the First has had his story told,
But there were Lords and Princes long before,

That had behav'd themselves like warriors bold;
Among the rest there was the great KING ARTHUR,
What hero's fame was ever carried farther?

IX.

King Arthur, and the Knights of his Round Table,

Were reckon'd the best King, and bravest Lords,
Of all that flourish'd since the Tower of Babel,

At least of all that history records;
Therefore I shall endeavour, if I'm able,

To paint their famous actions by my words:
Heroes exert themselves in hopes of Fame,
And having such a strong decisive claim,

X

It grieves me much, that Names that were respected
  In former ages, Persons of such mark,
And Countrymen of ours, should lie neglected,
  Just like old portraits lumbering in the dark :
An error such as this should be corrected,
  And if my Muse can strike a single spark,
Why then (as poets say) I'll string my lyre;
And then I'll light a great poetic Fire;

XI.

I'll air them all, and rub down the Round Table,
  And wash the Canvas clean, and scour the Frames,
And put a coat of varnish on the Fable,
  And try to puzzle out the Dates and Names;
Then (as I said before) I'll heave my cable,
  And take a pilot, and drop down the Thames—
—These first eleven stanzas make a Proem,
And now I must sit down and write my Poem.

I.

Beginning (as my Bookseller desires)

 Like an old Minstrel with his gown and beard,

" Fair Ladies, gallant Knights, and gentle Squires,

 " Now the last service from the Board is clear'd,

" And if this noble Company requires,

 " And if amidst your mirth I may be heard,

" Of sundry strange adventures I could tell,

" That oft were told before, but never told so well."

II.

THE GREAT KING ARTHUR made a sumptuous Feast,

 And held his Royal Christmas at Carlisle,

And thither came the Vassals, most and least,

 From every corner of this British Isle;

And all were entertain'd, both man and beast,

 According to their rank, in proper style;

The steeds were fed and litter'd in the stable,

The ladies and the knights sat down to table.

III.

The bill of fare (as you may well suppose)

 Was suited to those plentiful old times,

Before our modern luxuries arose,

 With truffles and ragouts, and various crimes;

And therefore, from the original in prose

 I shall arrange the catalogue in rhymes:

They serv'd up salmon, venison, and wild boars

By hundreds, and by dozens, and by scores.

IV.

Hogsheads of honey, kilderkins of mustard,

    Muttons, and fatted beeves, and bacon swine;

Herons and bitterns, peacock, swan and bustard,

    Teal, mallard, pigeons, widgeons, and in fine

Plum-puddings, pancakes, apple-pies and custard:

    And therewithal they drank good Gascon wine,

With mead, and ale, and cyder of our own;

For porter, punch, and negus, were not known.

V.

The noise and uproar of the scullery tribe,

    All pilfering and scrambling in their calling,

Was past all powers of language to describe—

    The din of manful oaths and female squalling:

The sturdy porter, huddling up his bribe,

    And then at random breaking heads and bawling,

Outcries, and cries of order, and contusions,

Made a confusion beyond all confusions;

VI.

Beggars and vagabonds, blind, lame, and sturdy,

    Minstrels and singers with their various airs,

The pipe, the tabor, and the hurdy-gurdy,

    Jugglers and mountebanks with apes and bears,

Continued from the first day to the third day,

    An uproar like ten thousand Smithfield fairs;

There were wild beasts and foreign birds and creatures,

And Jews and Foreigners with foreign features.

VII.

All sorts of people there were seen together,

    All sorts of characters, all sorts of dresses;

The fool with fox's tail and peacock's feather,

    Pilgrims, and penitents, and grave burgesses;

The country people with their coats of leather,

    Vintners and victuallers with cans and messes;

Grooms, archers, varlets, falconers and yeomen,

Damsels and waiting-maids, and waiting-women.

VIII.

But the profane, indelicate amours,

    The vulgar, unenlighten'd conversation

Of minstrels, menials, courtezans, and boors,

    (Although appropriate to their meaner station)

Would certainly revolt a taste like yours;

    Therefore I shall omit the calculation

Of all the curses, oaths, and cuts and stabs,

Occasion'd by their dice, and drink, and drabs.

IX.

We must take care in our poetic cruise,

    And never hold a single tack too long;

Therefore my versatile ingenious Muse

    Takes leave of this illiterate, low-bred throng,

Intending to present superior views,

    Which to genteeler company belong,

And show the higher orders of society

Behaving with politeness and propriety.

X.

And certainly they say, for fine behaving
    King Arthur's Court has never had its match;
True point of honour, without pride or braving,
    Strict etiquette for ever on the watch:
Their manners were refin'd and perfect—saving
    Some modern graces, which they could not catch,
As spitting through the teeth, and driving stages,
Accomplishments reserv'd for distant ages.

XI.

They look'd a manly, generous generation;
    Beards, shoulders, eyebrows, broad, and square, and
        thick,
Their accents firm and loud in conversation,
    Their eyes and gestures eager, sharp, and quick,
Shew'd them prepar'd, on proper provocation,
    To give the lie, pull noses, stab and kick;
And for that very reason, it is said,
They were so very courteous and well-bred.

XII.

The ladies look'd of an heroic race—

 At first a general likeness struck your eye,

Tall figures, open features, oval face,

 Large eyes, with ample eyebrows arch'd and high;

Their manners had an odd, peculiar grace,

 Neither repulsive, affable, nor shy,

Majestical, reserv'd, and somewhat sullen ;

Their dresses partly silk, and partly woollen.

XIII.

In form and figure far above the rest,

 Sir LAUNCELOT was chief of all the train,

In Arthur's Court an ever welcome guest;

 Britain will never see his like again.

Of all the Knights she ever had the best,

 Except, perhaps, Lord Wellington in Spain :

I never saw his picture nor his print,

From Morgan's Chronicle I take my hint.

XIV.

For Morgan says (at least as I have heard,

   And as a learned friend of mine assures),

Beside him all that lordly train appear'd

   Like courtly minions, or like common boors,

As if unfit for knightly deeds, and rear'd

   To rustic labours or to loose amours;

He mov'd amidst his peers without compare,

So lofty was his stature, look, and air.

XV.

Yet oftentimes his courteous cheer forsook

   His countenance, and then return'd again,

As if some secret recollection shook

   His inward heart with unacknowledged pain;

And something haggard in his eyes and look

   (More than his years or hardships could explain)

Made him appear, in person and in mind,

Less perfect than what nature had design'd.

XVI.

Of noble presence, but of different mien,

    Alert and lively, voluble and gay,

Sir TRISTRAM at Carlisle was rarely seen,

    But ever was regretted while away;

With easy mirth, an enemy to spleen,

    His ready converse charm'd the wintery day;

No tales he told of sieges or of fights,

Or foreign marvels, like the foolish Knights,

XVII.

But with a playful imitative tone

    (That merely seem'd a voucher for the truth)

Recounted strange adventures of his own,

    The chances of his childhood and his youth,

Of churlish Giants he had seen and known,

    Their rustic phrase and courtesies uncouth,

The dwellings, and the diet, and the lives

Of savage Monarchs and their monstrous Wives:

XVIII.

Songs, music, languages, and many a lay

    Asturian or Armoric, Irish, Basque,

His ready memory seiz'd and bore away;

    And ever when the Ladies chose to ask,

Sir Tristram was prepar'd to sing and play,

    Not like a minstrel earnest at his task,

But with a sportive, careless, easy style,

As if he seem'd to mock himself the while.

XIX.

His ready wit and rambling education,

    With the congenial influence of his stars,

Had taught him all the arts of conversation,

    All games of skill and stratagems of wars;

His birth, it seems, by Merlin's calculation,

    Was under Venus, Mercury, and Mars;

His mind with all their attributes was mixt,

And, like those planets, wandering and unfixt;

XX.

From realm to realm he ran—and never staid;

   Kingdoms and crowns he wan—and gave away:

It seem'd as if his labours were repaid

   By the mere noise and movement of the fray:

No conquests nor acquirements had he made:

   His chief delight was on some festive day

To ride triumphant, prodigal, and proud,

And shower his wealth amidst the shouting crowd:

XXI.

His schemes of war were sudden, unforeseen,

   Inexplicable both to friend and foe;

It seem'd as if some momentary spleen

   Inspir'd the project and impell'd the blow;

And most his fortune and success were seen

   With means the most inadequate and low;

Most master of himself, and least encumber'd

When overmatch'd, entangled, and outnumber'd.

c

XXII.

Strange instruments and engines he contriv'd

    For sieges, and constructions for defence,

Inventions some of them that have surviv'd,

    Others were deem'd too cumbrous and immense :

Minstrels he lov'd, and cherish'd while he liv'd,

    And patronized them both with praise and pence ;

Somewhat more learned than became a Knight,

It was reported he could read and write.

XXIII.

Sir GAWAIN may be painted in a word—

    He was a perfect loyal Cavalier ;

His courteous manners stand upon record,

    A stranger to the very thought of fear.

The proverb says, *As brave as his own sword ;*

    And like his weapon was that worthy Peer,

Of admirable temper, clear and bright,

Polish'd yet keen, though pliant yet upright.

XXIV.

On every point, in earnest or in jest,

    His judgment, and his prudence, and his wit,

Were deem'd the very touchstone and the test

    Of what was proper, graceful, just, and fit;

A word from him set every thing at rest,

    His short decisions never fail'd to hit;

His silence, his reserve, his inattention,

Were felt as the severest reprehension:

XXV.

His memory was the magazine and hoard,

    Where claims and grievances, from year to year,

And confidences and complaints were stor'd,

    From dame and knight, from damsel, boor, and peer:

Lov'd by his friends, and trusted by his Lord,

    A generous courtier, secret and sincere,

Adviser-general to the whole community,

He serv'd his friend, but watch'd his opportunity.

XXVI.

One riddle I could never understand—

    But his success in war was strangely various;

In executing schemes that others plann'd,

    He seem'd a very Cæsar or a Marius;

Take his own plans, and place him in command,

    Your prospect of success became precarious:

His plans were good, but Launcelot succeeded

And realized them better far than He did.

XXVII.

His discipline was stedfast and austere,

    Unalterably fix'd, but calm and kind;

Founded on admiration, more than fear,

    It seem'd an emanation from his mind;

The coarsest natures that approach'd him near

    Grew courteous for the moment and refin'd;

Beneath his eye the poorest, weakest wight

Felt full of point of honour like a knight.

XXVIII.

In battle he was fearless to a fault,

    The foremost in the thickest of the field ;

His eager valour knew no pause nor halt,

    And the red rampant Lion in his Shield

Scal'd Towns and Towers, the foremost in assault,

    With ready succour where the battle reel'd :

At random like a thunderbolt he ran,

And bore down shields, and pikes, and horse, and man.

CANTO II.

CANTO II.

I.

I've finish'd now three hundred lines and more,

   And therefore I begin Canto the Second,

Just like those wand'ring ancient Bards of Yore;

   They never laid a plan, nor ever reckon'd

What turning they should take the day before;

   They follow'd where the lovely Muses beckon'd:

The Muses led them up to Mount Parnassus,

And that's the reason that they all surpass us.

II.

The Muses serv'd those Heathens well enough—
 Bold Britons take a Tankard, or a Bottle,
And when the bottle's out, a pinch of snuff,
 And so proceed in spite of Aristotle—
Those Rules of his are dry, dogmatic stuff,
 All life and fire they suffocate and throttle—
And therefore I adopt the mode I mention,
Trusting to native judgment and invention.

III.

This method will, I hope, appear defensible—
 I shall begin by mentioning the Giants,
A race of mortals, brutal and insensible,
 (Postponing the details of the Defiance,
Which came in terms so very reprehensible
 From that barbarian sovereign King Ryence)
Displaying simpler manners, forms, and passions,
Unmix'd by transitory modes and fashions.

IV.

Before the Feast was ended, a Report

    Fill'd every soul with horror and dismay;

Some Ladies, on their journey to the Court,

    Had been surpris'd, and were convey'd away

By the Aboriginal Giants, to their Fort—

    An unknown Fort—for Government, they say,

Had ascertain'd its actual existence,

But knew not its direction, nor its distance.

V.

A waiting damsel, crooked and mis-shap'd,

    Herself the witness of a woful scene,

From which, by miracle, she had escap'd,

    Appear'd before the Ladies and the Queen;

Her figure was funereal, veil'd and crap'd,

    Her voice convuls'd with sobs and sighs between,

That with the sad recital, and the sight,

Revenge and rage inflam'd each worthy knight.

VI.

Sir Gawain rose without delay or dallying,

   "Excuse us, madam,—we've no time to waste—"

And at the palace-gate you saw him sallying,

   With other knights, equipp'd and armed in haste;

And there was Tristram making jests, and rallying

   The poor mis-shapen Damsel, whom he placed

Behind him on a pillion, pad, or pannel;

He took, besides, his falcon and his spaniel.

VII.

But what with horror, and fatigue, and fright,

   Poor soul, she could not recollect the way.

They reach'd the mountains on the second night,

   And wander'd up and down till break of day,

When they discover'd, by the dawning light,

   A lonely glen, where heaps of embers lay;

They found unleaven'd fragments, scorch'd and toasted,

And the remains of mules and horses roasted.

VIII.

Sir Tristram understood the Giants' courses—

    He felt the embers, but the heat was out—

He stood contemplating the roasted horses,

    And all at once, without suspense or doubt,

His own decided judgment thus enforces—

    " The Giants must be somewhere here about !"

Demonstrating the carcasses, he shows

That they remain'd untouch'd by kites or crows ;

IX.

" You see no traces of their sleeping here,

    " No heap of leaves or heath, no Giant's nest—

" Their usual habitation must be near—

    " They feed at sunset, and retire to rest—

" A moment's search will set the matter clear."

    The fact turn'd out precisely as he guess'd ;

And shortly after, scrambling through a gully,

He verified his own conjecture fully.

X.

He found a Valley, closed on every side,

    Resembling that which Rasselas* describes;

Six miles in length, and half as many wide,

    Where the descendants of the Giant tribes

Liv'd in their ancient Fortress undescried:

    (Invaders tread upon each others kibes)

First came the Britons, afterwards the Roman,

Our patrimonial lands belong to no man:

XI.

So Horace said—and so the Giants found,

    Expelled by fresh invaders in succession;

But they maintain'd tenaciously the ground

    Of ancient, indefeasible possession,

And robb'd and ransack'd all the country round;

    And ventur'd on this horrible transgression,

Claiming a right reserv'd to waste and spoil,

As Lords and lawful owners of the soil.

        * Prince of Abyssinia.   See his Life, written by himself.

XII.

Huge mountains of immeasurable height

    Encompass'd all the level Valley round,

With mighty slabs of rock, that slop'd upright,

    An insurmountable, enormous mound ;

The very River vanish'd out of sight,

    Absorb'd in secret channels under ground :

That Vale was so sequester'd and secluded,

All search for ages past it had eluded.

XIII.

High over head was many a Cave and Den,

    That with its strange construction seem'd to mock

All thought of how they were contriv'd, or when—

    —Hewn inward in the huge suspended Rock,

The Tombs and Monuments of mighty men :

    Such were the patriarchs of this ancient stock.

Alas ! what pity that the present race

Should be so barbarous, and deprav'd, and base !

XIV.

For they subsisted (as I said) by pillage,

    And the wild beasts which they pursu'd and chas'd :

Nor house, nor herdsman's hut, nor farm, nor village,

    Within the lonely valley could be traced,

Nor roads, nor bounded fields, nor rural tillage,

    But all was lonely, desolate, and waste.

The Castle which commanded the domain

Was suited to so rude and wild a Reign :

XV.

A Rock was in the centre, like a Cone,

    Abruptly rising from a miry pool,

Where they beheld a Pile of massy stone,

    Which masons of the rude primæval school

Had rear'd by help of Giant hands alone,

    With rocky fragments unreduc'd by rule,

Irregular, like Nature more than Art,

Huge, rugged, and compact in every part.

XVI.

But on the other side a River went,

 And there the craggy Rock and ancient Wall

Had crumbled down with shelving deep descent;

 Time and the wearing stream had work'd its fall:

The modern Giants had repair'd the Rent,

 But poor, reduc'd, and ignorant withal,

They patch'd it up, contriving as they could,

With stones, and earth, and palisades of wood;

XVII.

Sir Gawain tried a parley, but in vain—

A true bred Giant never trusts a Knight—

He sent a Herald, who return'd again

 All torn to rags and perishing with fright;

A Trumpeter was sent, but he was slain—

 To Trumpeters they bear a mortal spite:

When all conciliatory measures fail'd,

The Castle and the Fortress were assail'd.

XVIII.

But when the Giants saw them fairly under,

   They shovell'd down a cataract of stones,

A hideous volley like a peal of thunder,

   Bouncing and bounding down, and breaking bones,

Rending the earth, and riving rocks asunder;

   Sir Gawain inwardly laments and groans,

Retiring last, and standing most expos'd;—

Success seem'd hopeless, and the combat clos'd.

XIX.

A Council then was call'd, and all agreed

   To call in succour from the Country round;

By regular approaches to proceed,

   Intrenching, fortifying, breaking ground.

That morning Tristram happen'd to secede:

   It seems his Falcon was not to be found;

He went in search of her, but some suspected

He went lest his advice should be neglected.

XX.

At Gawain's summons all the Country came;

　At Gawain's summons all the people aided;

They called upon each other in his name,

　And bid their neighbours work as hard as they did.

So well belov'd was He, for very shame

　They dug, they delv'd, entrench'd, and palisaded,

Till all the Fort was thoroughly blockaded,

And every Ford where Giants might have waded.

XXI.

Sir Tristram found his Falcon, bruis'd and lame,

　After a tedious search, as he averr'd,

And was returning back the way he came

　When in the neighbouring thicket something stirr'd,

And flash'd across the path, as bright as flame,

　Sir Tristram follow'd it, and found a Bird

Much like a Pheasant, only crimson red,

With a fine tuft of feathers on his head.

XXII.

Sir Tristram's mind—invention—pow'rs of thought,

Were occupied, abstracted, and engag'd,

Devising ways and means to have it caught

Alive—entire—to see it safely cag'd:

The Giants and their siege he set at nought

Compar'd with this new warfare that he wag'd.

He gain'd his object after three days wandering,

And three nights watching, meditating, pondering,

XXIII.

And to the Camp in triumph he return'd:

He makes them all admire the creature's crest,

And praise and magnify the prize he earn'd.

Sir Gawain rarely ventur'd on a jest,

But here his heart with indignation burn'd:—

" Good Cousin, yonder stands an Eagle's nest!

—" A Prize for Fowlers such as you and me."—

Sir Tristram answer'd mildly, " We shall see."

XXIV.

Good humour was Sir Tristram's leading quality,

    And in the present case he prov'd it such;

If he forbore, it was that in reality

    His conscience smote him with a secret touch,

For having shock'd his worthy friend's formality—

    He thought Sir Gawain had not said too much;

'He walks apart with him—and he discourses

About their preparation and their forces—

XXV.

Approving every thing that had been done—

    " It serves to put the Giants off their guard—

" Less hazard and less danger will be run—

    " I doubt not we shall find them unprepar'd—

" The Castle will more easily be won,

    " And many valuable lives be spar'd;

" The Ladies else, while we blockade and threaten,

" Will most infallibly be kill'd and eaten."

XXVI.

Sir Tristram talk'd incomparably well;

   His reasons were irrefragably strong.
As Tristram spoke Sir Gawain's spirits fell,

   For he discover'd clearly before long
(What Tristram never would presume to tell),

   That his whole system was entirely wrong;
In fact his confidence had much diminish'd
Since all the preparations had been finish'd.

XXVII.

" Indeed!" Sir Tristram said, " for ought we know—

   " For ought that we can tell—this very night
" The valley's entrance may be clos'd with snow,

   " And we may starve and perish here outright—
" 'Tis better risking a decided blow—

   " I own this weather puts me in a fright."
In fine, this tedious conference to shorten,
Sir Gawain trusted to Sir Tristram's fortune.

XXVIII.

'Twas twilight, ere the wint'ry dawn had kist
  With cold salute the mountain's chilly brow;
The level lawns were dark, a lake of mist
  Inundated the vales and depths below,
When valiant Tristram, with a chosen list
  Of bold and hardy men, prepar'd to go,
Ascending through the vapours dim and hoar,
A secret track, which he descried before.

XXIX.

If ever you attempted, when a boy,
  To walk across the play-ground or the yard
Blindfolded, for an apple or a toy,
  Which, when you reach'd the spot, was your reward,
You may conceive the difficult employ
  Sir Tristram had, and that he found it hard,
Depriv'd of landmarks and the power of sight,
To steer their dark and doubtful course aright.

XXX.

They climb'd an hour or more with hand and knee

   (The distance of a fathom or a rood

Was farther than the keenest eye could see;)

   At last the very ground on which they stood,

The broken turf, and many a batter'd tree—

   The crush'd and shatter'd shrubs and underwood—

Apprized them that they were arriv'd once more

Where they were overwhelm'd the time before.

XXXI.

Sir Tristram saw the people in a fluster;

   He took them to a shelter'd hollow place:

They crowded round like chickens in a cluster,

   And Tristram, with an unembarrass'd face,

Proceeded quietly to take a muster,

   To take a muster, and to state the case—

" It was," he said, " an unexpected error,

" Enough to strike inferior minds with terror;

XXXII.

" But since they were assembled and collected,"

   (All were assembled except nine or ten)

" He thought that their design might be effected ;

   " All things were easy to determin'd men.

" If they would take the track which he directed,

   " And try their old adventure once again,"

He slapp'd his breast, and swore within an hour

That they should have the Castle in their power.

XXXIII.

This mountain was like others I have seen ;

   There was a stratum or a ridge of stone

Projecting high beyond the sloping green,

   From top to bottom, like a spinal bone,

Or flight of steps, with gaps and breaks between—

   A Copper-plate would make my meaning known

Better than words, and therefore, with permission,

I'll give a Print of it the next Edition.

XXXIV.

Thither Sir Tristram with his comrades went,
  For now the misty cloud was clear'd away,
And they must risk the perilous ascent,
  Right in the Giants' front, in open day:
They ran to reach the shelter which it lent,
  Before the battery should begin to play.
Their manner of ascending up that ridge
Was much like climbing by a broken bridge;

XXXV.

For there you scramble on from pier to pier,
  Always afraid to lose your hold half way;
And as they clamber'd each successive tier
  Of rugged upright rocks, I dare to say,
It was not altogether without fear—
  Just fear enough to make brave people gay:
According to the words of Mr. Gray,
" They wound with toilsome march their long array."

XXXVI.

The more alert and active upward sprung,

    And let down ropes to drag their comrades after;

Those ropes were their own shirts together strung,

    Stript off and twisted with such mirth and laughter,

That with their jokes the rocky echoes rung:

    Like countrymen that on a beam or rafter

Attempt to pass a raging wintry flood,

Such was the situation where they stood:

XXXVII.

A wild tumultuous torrent rag'd around,

    Of fragments tumbling from the mountain's height;

The whirling clouds of dust, the deafening sound,

    The hurried motion that amazed the sight,

The constant quaking of the solid ground,

    Environ'd them with phantoms of affright;

Yet with heroic hearts they held right on,

Till the last point of their ascent was won.

XXXVIII.

The Giants saw them on the topmost crown

    Of the last rock, and threaten'd and defied—

" Down with the mangy dwarfs there!—Dash them down!

    Down with the dirty pismires!"—Thus they cried.

Sir Tristram, with a sharp sarcastic frown,

    In their own Giant jargon thus replied,

" Mullinger!—Cacamole!—and Mangonell!

" You cursed cannibals—I know you well—

XXXIX.

" I'll see that pate of yours upon a post,

    " And your left-handed squinting brother's too—

" By Heaven and Earth, within an hour at most,

    " I'll give the crows a meal of him and you—

" The wolves shall have you—either raw or roast—

    " I'll make an end of all your cursed crew."

These words he partly said, and partly sang,

As usual with the Giants, in their slang.

XL.

He darted forward to the mountain's brow—
    The Giants ran away—they knew not why—
Sir Tristram gained the point—he knew not how—
    He could account for it no more than I.
Such strange effects we witness often now;
    Such strange experiments true Britons try
In sieges, and in skirmishes afloat,
In storming heights, and boarding from a boat.

XLI.

True Courage bears about a Charm or Spell—
    It looks, I think, like an instinctive Law
By which superior natures daunt and quell
    Frenchmen and foreigners with fear and awe.
I wonder if Philosophers can tell—
    Can they explain the thing with all their jaw?
I can't explain it—but the fact is so,
A fact which every midshipman must know.

XLII.

Then instantly the signal was held out,

    To shew Sir Gawain that the coast was clear :

They heard his Camp re-echo with a shout—

    In half an hour Sir Gawain will be here.

But still Sir Tristram was perplext with doubt—

    The crisis of the Ladies' fate drew near—

He dreaded what those poor defenceless creatures

Might suffer from such fierce and desperate natures.

XLIII.

The Giants, with their brutal want of sense,

    In hurling stones to crush them with the fall,

And in their hurry taking them from thence,

    Had half dismantled all the new-built Wall.

They left it here and there, a naked fence

    Of stakes and palisades, upright and tall.

Sir Tristram form'd a sudden resolution,

And recommended it for execution.

XLIV.

" My Lads," he cried, " an effort must be made

" To keep those Monsters half an hour in play,

" While Gawain is advancing to our aid,

" Or else the Ladies will be made away.

" By mounting close within the palisade,

" You'll parry their two-handed, dangerous sway—

" Their Clubs and Maces : recollect my words,

" And use your daggers rather than your swords."

XLV.

That service was most gallantly perform'd :

The Giants still endeavour'd to repel

And drive them from the breach that they had storm'd :

The foremost of the Crew was Mangonell.

At sight of him Sir Tristram's spirit warm'd ;

With aim unerring Tristram's faulchion fell,

Lopt off his Club and fingers at the knuckle,

And thus disabled that stupendous Chuckle.

XLVI.

The Giant ran, outrageous with the wound,

 Roaring and bleeding, to the palisade;

Sir Tristram swerv'd aside, and reaching round,

 Prob'd all his entrails with his poniard's blade:

His Giant limbs fall thundering on the ground,

 His goggling eyes eternal slumbers shade;

Then by the head or heels, I know not which,

They dragg'd him forth, and tost him in the Ditch.

XLVII.

Sir Tristram, in the warfare that he wag'd,

 Strove to attract the Giants' whole attention;

To keep it undivided and engag'd,

 He rack'd his fiery brain and his invention;

And taunted and revil'd, and storm'd, and rag'd,

 In terms far worse, and more than I can mention.

In the mean while, in a more sober manner,

Sir Gawain was advancing with his banner.

XLVIII.

But first I must commemorate in Rhime

    Sir Tristram's dext'rous swordmanship and might,

(This incident appears to me sublime),

    He struck a Giant's head off in the fight:

The head fell down of course, but for some time

    The stupid, headless trunk remain'd upright;

For more than twenty seconds there it stood,

But ultimately fell from loss of blood.

XLIX.

Behold Sir Gawain with his valiant band;

    He enters on the work with warmth and haste,

And slays a brace of Giants out of hand,

    Slic'd downward from the shoulder to the waist.

But our ichnography must now be plann'd,

    The Keep or Inner Castle must be trac'd.

I wish myself at the concluding distich,

Although I think the thing characteristic.

E

L.

Facing your Entrance, just three yards behind,

    There was a Mass of Stone of moderate height,

It stood before you like a screen or blind:

    And there—on either hand to left and right—

Were sloping Parapets or Planes inclin'd,

    On which two massy Stones were plac'd upright,

Secured by Staples and by leathern Ropes,

Which hinder'd them from sliding down the slopes.

LI.

" —Cousin, those Dogs have some device or gin !—

    " —I'll run the gauntlet—and I'll stand a knock—"

He dash'd into the Gate through thick and thin—

    He hew'd away the bands which held the block—

It rush'd along the slope with rumbling din,

    And closed the entrance with a thundering shock,

(Just like those famous old Symplegades

Discover'd by the Classics in their seas.)

LII.

This was Sir Tristram—(as you may suppose)

He found some Giants wounded, others dead—
He shortly equalizes these with those;

But one poor Devil there was sick in bed,
In whose behalf the Ladies interpose;

Sir Tristram spar'd his life, because they said
That he was more humane, and mild, and clever,
And all the time had had an ague-fever.

LIII.

The Ladies?—They were tolerably well,

At least as well as could have been expected:
Many details I must forbear to tell,

Their toilet had been very much neglected;
But by supreme good luck it so befell

That when the Castle's capture was effected,
When those vile cannibals were overpower'd,
Only two fat Duennas were devour'd.

LIV.

Sir Tristram having thus secur'd the Fort,

    And seen all safe, was climbing to the Wall,

(Meaning to leap into the outer Court;)

    But when he came, he sav'd himself the fall,

Sir Gawain had been spoiling all the sport,

    The Giants were demolish'd one and all:

He pull'd them up the Wall—they climb and enter—

Such was the winding up of this adventure.

LV.

The only real sufferer in the fight

    Was a poor neighbouring Squire of little fame,

That came and join'd the party over-night;

    He hobbled home, disabled with a maim

Which he receiv'd in tumbling from a height:

    The Knights from Court had never heard his name,

Nor recollected seeing him before—

Two leopards' faces were the arms he bore.

LVI.

Thus Tristram, without loss of life or limb,

 Conquer'd the Giants' Castle in a day;

But whether it were accident or whim

 That kept him in the Woods so long away,

In any other mortal except him

 I should not feel a doubt of what to say;

But he was wholly guided by his humour,

Indifferent to report and public rumour.

LVII.

It was besides imagined and suspected

 That he had miss'd his course by deep design,

To take the track which Gawain had neglected—

 I speak of others' notions, not of mine:

I question even if he recollected—

 He might have felt a moment's wish to shine;

I only know that he made nothing of it,

Either for reputation or for profit.

LVIII.

The Ladies, by Sir Gawain's kind direction,

    Proceeded instantaneously to Court,

To thank their Majesties for their protection.

    Sir Gawain follow'd with a grand escort,

And was received with favour and affection.

    Sir Tristram remain'd loitering in the Fort;

He thought the building and the scenery striking,

And that poor captive Giant took his liking.

LIX.

And now the thread of our Romance unravels,

    Presenting new performers on the stage;

A Giant's education and his travels

    Will occupy the next succeeding page:

But I begin to tremble at the cavils

    Of this fastidious, supercilious age;

Reviews, and paragraphs in morning papers—

The prospect of them gives my Muse the vapours.

LX.

" My dear," says she, " I think it will be well

   " To ascertain our losses or our gains:

" If this first sample should succeed and sell,

   " We can renew the same melodious strains."

Poor soul! she's had, I think, a tedious spell,

   And ought to be consider'd for her pains.

And keeping of my company so long—

A moderate compliment would not be wrong.

THE END.

T Davison, Lombard-street,
Whitefriars, London.

PROSPECTUS AND SPECIMEN

OF AN INTENDED

National Work,

BY

WILLIAM AND ROBERT WHISTLECRAFT,

OF STOW-MARKET, IN SUFFOLK, HARNESS AND COLLAR-MAKERS.

INTENDED TO COMPRISE

THE MOST INTERESTING PARTICULARS

RELATING TO

King Arthur and his Round Table.

CANTOS III. AND IV.

LONDON:

JOHN MURRAY, ALBEMARLE-STREET.

1818.

CANTO III.

―――

I.

' I've a proposal here from Mr. Murray,

    ' He offers handsomely—the money down;

' My dear, you might recover from your flurry

    ' In a nice airy lodging out of town,

' At Croydon, Epsom, any where in Surry;

    ' If every stanza brings us in a crown,

' I think that I might venture to bespeak

' A bed-room and front parlour for next week.

II.

' Tell me, my dear Thalia, what you think;

  ' Your nerves have undergone a sudden shock ;

' Your poor dear spirits have begun to sink ;

  ' On Banstead Downs you'd muster a new stock,

' And I'd be sure to keep away from drink,

  ' And always go to bed by twelve o'clock.

' We'll travel down there in the morning stages ;

' Our verses shall go down to distant ages.

III.

' And here in town we'll breakfast on hot rolls,

  ' And you shall have a better shawl to wear;

' These pantaloons of mine are chaf'd in holes ;

  ' By Monday next I'll compass a new pair:

' Come, now, fling up the cinders, fetch the coals,

  ' And take away the things you hung to air,

' Set out the tea-things, and bid Phœbe bring

' The kettle up.'—*Arms and the Monks I sing.*

IV.

Some ten miles off, an ancient abbey stood,

　　Amidst the mountains, near a noble stream;

A level eminence, enshrin'd with wood,

　　Slop'd to the river's bank and southern beam;

Within were fifty friars fat and good,

　　Of goodly persons, and of good esteem,

That pass'd an easy, exemplary life,

Remote from want and care, and worldly strife.

V.

Between the Monks and Giants there subsisted,

　　In the first abbot's lifetime, much respect;

The Giants let them settle where they listed;

　　The Giants were a tolerating sect.

A poor lame Giant once the Monks assisted,

　　Old and abandon'd, dying with neglect,

The Prior found him, cur'd his broken bone,

And very kindly cut him for the stone.

VI.

This seem'd a glorious, golden opportunity,

    To civilize the whole gigantic race ;

To draw them to pay tythes, and dwell in unity ;

    The Giants' valley was a fertile place,

And might have much enrich'd the whole community,

    Had the old Giant liv'd a longer space ;

But he relaps'd, and though all means were tried,

They could but just baptize him—when he died.

VII.

And, I believe, the Giants never knew

    Of the kind treatment that befel their mate ;

He broke down all at once, and all the crew

    Had taken leave, and left him to his fate ;

And though the Monks expos'd him full in view,

    Propp'd on his crutches, at the garden gate,

To prove their cure, and shew that all was right,

It happen'd that no Giants came in sight :

VIII.

They never found another case to cure,

    But their demeanour calm and reverential,
Their gesture and their vesture grave and pure,

    Their conduct sober, cautious, and prudential,
Engag'd respect, sufficient to secure

    Their properties and interests most essential;
They kept a distant, courteous intercourse;
Salutes and gestures were their sole discourse.

IX.

Music will civilize, the poets say,

    In time it might have civiliz'd the Giants;
The Jesuits found its use in Paraguay;

    Orpheus was famous for harmonic science,
And civilized the Thracians in that way;

    My judgment coincides with Mr. Bryant's;
He thinks that Orpheus meant a race of cloisterers,
Obnoxious to the Bacchanalian roisterers.

X.

Decyphering the symbols of mythology,

    He finds them Monks, expert in their vocation ;

Teachers of music, med'cine, and theology,

    The missionaries of the barbarous Thracian ;

The poet's fable was a wild apology

    For an inhuman bloody reformation,

Which left those tribes unciviliz'd and rude,

Naked and fierce, and painted and tattoo'd.

XI.

It was a glorious Jacobinic job

    To pull down convents, to condemn for treason

Poor peeping Pentheus—to carouse and rob,

    With naked raving goddesses of reason,

The festivals and orgies of the mob

    That every twentieth century come in season.

Enough of Orpheus—the succeeding page

Relates to Monks of a more recent age ;

XII.

And oft that wild untutor'd race would draw,

    Led by the solemn sound and sacred light

Beyond the bank, beneath a lonely shaw,

    To listen all the livelong summer night,

Till deep, serene, and reverential awe

    Environ'd them with silent calm delight,

Contemplating the Minster's midnight gleam,

Reflected from the clear and glassy stream;

XIII.

But chiefly, when the shadowy moon had shed

    O'er woods and waters her mysterious hue,

Their passive hearts and vacant fancies fed

    With thoughts and aspirations strange and new,

Till their brute souls with inward working bred

    Dark hints that in the depth of instinct grew

Subjèctive—not from Locke's associations,

Nor David Hartley's doctrine of vibrations.

XIV.

Each was asham'd to mention to the others

One half of all the feelings that he felt,

Yet thus far each could venture—' Listen, brothers,

' It seems as if one heard heaven's thunder melt

' In music—! all at once it sooths—it smothers—

' It overpow'rs one—Pillicock, don't pelt !

' It seems a kind of shame, a kind of sin,

' To vex those harmless worthy souls within,'

XV.

In castles and in courts Ambition dwells,

But not in castles or in courts alone ;

She breath'd a wish, throughout those sacred cells,

For bells of larger size, and louder tone ;

Giants abominate the sound of bells,

And soon the fierce antipathy was shown,

The tinkling and the jingling, and the clangor,

Rous'd their irrational gigantic anger.

XVI.

Unhappy mortals! ever blind to fate!

    Unhappy Monks! you see no danger nigh;
Exulting in their sound and size and weight,

    From morn till noon the merry peal you ply:
The belfry rocks, your bosoms are elate,

    Your spirits with the ropes and pullies fly;
Tir'd, but transported, panting, pulling, hauling,
Ramping and stamping, overjoy'd and bawling.

XVII.

Meanwhile the solemn mountains that surrounded

    The silent valley where the convent lay,
With tintinnabular uproar were astounded,

    When the first peal burst forth at break of day:
Feeling their granite ears severely wounded,

    They scarce knew what to think, or what to say;
And (though large mountains commonly conceal
Their sentiments, dissembling what they feel,

XVIII.

Yet) Cader-Gibbrish from his cloudy throne

    To huge Loblommon gave an intimation

Of this strange rumour, with an awful tone,

    Thund'ring his deep surprise and indignation;

The lesser hills, in language of their own,

    Discuss'd the topic by reverberation;

Discoursing with their echoes all day long,

Their only conversation was, ' ding-dong.'

XIX.

Those giant-mountains inwardly were mov'd,

    But never made an outward change of place:

Not so the mountain-giants—(as behov'd

    A more alert and locomotive race),

Hearing a clatter which they disapprov'd,

    They ran straight forward to besiege the place

With a discordant universal yell,

Like house-dogs howling at a dinner-bell.

XX.

Historians are extremely to be pitied,

   Oblig'd to persevere in the narration

Of wrongs and horrid outrages committed,

   Oppression, sacrilege, assassination;

The following scenes I wish'd to have omitted,

   But truth is an imperious obligation.

So—' my heart sickens, and I drop my pen,'

And am oblig'd to pick it up again,

XXI.

And, dipping it afresh, I must transcribe

   An ancient monkish record, which displays

The savage acts of that gigantic tribe;

   I hope, that from the diction of those days,

This noble, national poem will imbibe

   A something (in the old reviewing phrase),

' Of an original flavour, and a raciness;'

I should not else transcribe it out of laziness.

XXII.

The writer first relates a dream, or vision,

    Observ'd by Luke and Lawrence in their cells,

And a nocturnal hideous apparition

    Of fiends and devils dancing round the bells:

This last event is stated with precision;

    Their persons he describes, their names he tells,

Klaproth, Tantallan, Barbanel, Belphegor,

Long-tail'd, long-talon'd, hairy, black, and meagre.

XXIII.

He then rehearses sundry marvels more,

    Damping the mind with horror by degrees,

Of a prodigious birth a heifer bore,

    Of mermaids seen in the surrounding seas,

Of a sea-monster that was cast ashore;

    Earthquakes and thunder-stones, events like these,

Which serv'd to shew the times were out of joint,

And then proceeds directly to the point.

XXIV.

Erant rumores et timores varii;

  Dies horroris et confusionis

Evenit in calendis Januarii;

  Gigantes, semen maledictionis

Nostri potentes impii adversarii,

  Irascebantur campanarum sonis,

Horâ secundâ centum tres gigantes

Venerunt ante januam ululantes.

XXV.

At fratres pleni desolationis,

  Stabant ad necessarium præsidium,

Perterriti pro vitis et pro bonis,

  Et perduravit hoc crudele obsidium,

Nostri claustralis pauperis Sionis,

  Ad primum diem proximorum Idium;

Tunc in triumpho fracto tintinnabulo,

Gigantes ibant alibi pro pabulo.

XXVI.

Sed frater Isidorus decumbebat

   In lecto per tres menses brachio fracto,

Nam lapides Mangonellus jaciebat,

   Et fregit tintinnabulum lapide jacto;

Et omne vicinagium destruebat,

   Et nihil relinquebat de intacto,

Ardens molinos, Casas, messuagia,

Et alia multa damna atque outragia.

XXVII.

Those Monks were poor proficients in divinity,

   And scarce knew more of Latin than myself;

Compar'd with theirs they say that true Latinity

   Appears like porcelain compar'd with delf;

As for the damage done in the vicinity,

   Those that have laid their Latin on the shelf

May like to read the subsequent narration

Done into metre from a friend's translation.

XXVIII.

Squire Humphry Bamberham, of Boozley Hall,

 (Whose name I mention with deserv'd respect),

On market-days was often pleas'd to call,

 And to suggest improvements, or correct;

I own the obligation once for all,

 Lest critics should imagine they detect

Traces of learning and superior reading,

Beyond, as they suppose, my birth and breeding.

XXIX.

Papers besides, and transcripts most material,

 He gave me when I went to him to dine;

A trunk full, one coach-seat, and an imperial,

 One band-box—But the work is wholly mine;

The tone, the form, the colouring etherial,

 ' The vision and the faculty divine,'

The scenery, characters, and triple-rhymes,

I'll swear it—like old Walter of the Times.

XXX.

Long, long before, upon a point of weight,

    Such as a ring of bells complete and new,

Chapters were summon'd, frequent, full, and late;

    The point was view'd in every point of view,

Till, after fierce discussion and debate,

    The wiser monks, the wise are always few,

That from the first oppos'd the plan *in toto*,

Were over-borne, *canonicali voto.*

XXXI.

A prudent monk, their reader and librarian,

    Observ'd a faction, angry, strong, and warm,

(Himself an anti-tintinnabularian),

    He saw, or thought he saw, a party form

To scout him as an alien and sectarian.

    There was an undefin'd impending storm!

The opponents were united, bold, and hot;

They might degrade, imprison him—what not?

XXXII.

Now faction in a city, camp, or cloister,

 While it is yet a tender raw beginner,

Is nourish'd by superfluous warmth and moisture,

 Namely, by warmth and moisture after dinner;

And therefore, till the temper and the posture

 Of things should alter—till a secret inner

Instinctive voice should whisper, all is right—

He deem'd it safest to keep least in sight.

XXXIII.

He felt as if his neck were in a noose,

 And evermore retir'd betimes from table,

For fear of altercation and abuse,

 But made the best excuse that he was able;

He never rose without a good excuse,

 (Like Master Stork invited in the fable

To Mr. Fox's dinner); there he sat,

Impatient to retire and take his hat.

c

XXXIV.

For only once or twice that he remain'd

   To change this constant formal course, he found

His brethren awkward, sullen, and constrain'd,

   —He caught the conversation at a bound,

And, with a hurried agitation, strain'd

   His wits to keep it up, and drive it round.

—It sav'd him—but he felt the risk and danger,

Behav'd-to like a pleasant utter stranger.

XXXV.

Wise people sometimes will pretend to sleep,

   And watch and listen while they droop and snore—

He felt himself a kind of a black sheep,

   But studied to be neither less nor more

Obliging than became him—but to keep

   His temper, stile, and manner as before;

It seem'd the best, the safest, only plan,

Never to seem to feel as a mark'd man.

XXXVI.

Wise Curs, when canister'd, refuse to run ;

 They merely crawl and creep about, and whine,

And disappoint the Boys, and spoil the fun—

 That picture is too mean—this Monk of mine

Ennobled it, as others since have done,

 With grace and ease, and grandeur of design;

He neither ran nor howl'd, nor crept nor turn'd,

But wore it as he walk'd, quite unconcern'd.

XXXVII.

To manifest the slightest want of nerve

 Was evidently perfect, utter ruin,

Therefore the seeming to recant or swerve,

 By meddling any way with what was doing,

He felt within himself would only serve

 To bring down all the mischief that was brewing ;

" No duty binds me, no constraint compels

" To bow before the Dagon of the Bells,

XXXVIII.

" To flatter this new foolery, to betray

 " My vote, my conscience, and my better sense,

" By bustling in the Belfry day by day;

 " But in the Grange, the Cellar, or the Spence,

" (While all are otherwise employ'd), I may

 " Deserve their thanks, at least avoid offence;

" For (while this vile anticipated clatter

 " Fills all their hearts and senses), every matter

XXXIX.

" Behoveful for our maintenance and needs

 " Is wholly disregarded, and the course

" Of our conventual management proceeds

 " At random, day by day, from bad to worse;

" The Larder dwindles and the Cellar bleeds!

 " Besides,—besides the bells, we must disburse

" For masonry, for frame-work, wheels and fliers;

" Next winter we must fast like genuine friars."

XL.

As Bees, that when the skies are calm and fair,
  In June, or the beginning of July,
Launch forth colonial settlers in the air,
  Round, round, and round-about, they whiz, they fly,
With eager worry whirling here and there,
  They know not whence, nor whither, where, nor why,
In utter hurry-scurry, going, coming,
Maddening the summer air with ceaseless humming;

XLI.

Till the strong Frying-pan's energic jangle
  With thrilling thrum their feebler hum doth drown,
Then passive and appeas'd, they droop and dangle,
  Clinging together close, and clust'ring down,
Link'd in a multitudinous living tangle
  Like an old Tassel of a dingy brown;
The joyful Farmer sees, and spreads his hay,
And reckons on a settled sultry day.

XLII.

E'en so the Monks, as wild as sparks of fire,

  (Or swarms unpacified by pan or kettle),

Ran restless round the Cloisters and the Quire,

  Till those huge masses of sonorous metal

Attracted them toward the Tower and Spire;

  There you might see them cluster, crowd, and settle,

Throng'd in the hollow tintinnabular Hive;

The Belfry swarm'd with Monks; it seem'd alive.

XLIII.

Then, while the Cloisters, Courts, and Yards were still,

  Silent and empty, like a long vacation;

The Friar prowl'd about, intent to fill

  Details of delegated occupation,

Which, with a ready frankness and good will,

  He undertook; he said, " the obligation

" Was nothing—nothing—he could serve their turn

" While they were busy with this new concern."

XLIV.

Combining prudence with a scholar's pride,
    Poor Tully, like a toad beneath a harrow,
Twitch'd, jerk'd, and haul'd and maul'd on every side,
    Tried to identify himself with Varro;
This course our cautious Friar might have tried,
    But his poor convent was a field too narrow;
There was not, from the Prior to the Cook,
A single soul that car'd about a book:

XLV.

Yet, sitting with his books, he felt unclogg'd,
    Unfetter'd; and for hours together tasted
The calm delight of being neither dogg'd,
    Nor watch'd, nor worried; he transcribed, he pasted,
Repaired old Bindings, index'd, catalogued,
    Illuminated, mended Clasps, and wasted
An hour or two sometimes in actual reading;
Meanwhile the belfry business was proceeding;

XLVI.

And the first opening Peal, the grand display,

    In prospect ever present to his mind,

Was fast approaching, pregnant with dismay,

    With loathing and with horror undefin'd,

Like th' expectation of an Ague-day;

    The day before he neither supp'd nor din'd,

And felt beforehand, for a fortnight near,

A kind of deafness in his fancy's ear:

XLVII.

But most he fear'd his ill digested spleen,

    Inflam'd by gibes, might lead him on to wrangle,

Or discompose, at least, his looks and mien;

    So, with the Belfry's first prelusive jangle,

He sallied from the Garden-gate unseen,

    With his worst hat, his boots, his line and angle,

Meaning to pass away the time, and bring

Some fish for supper, as a civil thing.

XLVIII.

The prospect of their after-supper talk

   Employ'd his thoughts, forecasting many a scoff,

Which he with quick reply must damp and balk,

   Parrying at once, without a hem or cough,

" Had not the bells annoy'd him in his walk?—

   " No, faith! he lik'd them best when farthest off."

Thus he prepar'd and practis'd many a sentence,

Expressing ease, good-humour, independence.

XLIX.

His ground-bait had been laid the night before,

   Most fortunately!—for he us'd to say,

' That more than once the belfry's bothering roar

   ' Almost induc'd him to remove away;'

Had he so done,—the gigantean corps

   Had sack'd the convent on that very day,

But providentially the perch and dace

Bit freely, which detain'd him at the place.

L.

And here let us detain ourselves awhile,

    My dear Thalia ! party's angry frown

And petty malice in that monkish pile,

    (The warfare of the cowl and of the gown),

Had almost dried my wits and drain'd my style ;

    Here, with our legs, then, idly dangling down,

We'll rest upon the bank, and dip our toes

In the poetic current as it flows.

LI.

Or in the narrow sunny plashes near,

    Observe the puny piscatory Swarm,

That with their tiny Squadrons tack and veer,

    Cruizing amidst the shelves and shallows warm,

Chasing, or in retreat, with hope or fear

    Of petty plunder or minute alarm ;

With clannish instinct how they wheel and face,

Inherited arts inherent in the race ;

LII.

Or mark the jetty, glossy Tribes that glance
   Upon the water's firm unruffled breast,
Tracing their ancient labyrinthic dance
   In mute mysterious cadence unexpress'd;
Alas! that fresh disaster and mischance
   Again must drive us from our place of rest!
Grim Mangonel, with his outrageous crew,
Will scare us hence within an hour or two.

LIII.

Poets are privileg'd to run away—
   Alcæus and Archilochus could fling
Their shields behind them in a doubtful fray;
   And still sweet Horace may be heard to sing
His filthy fright upon Philippi's day;
   (—You can retire, too—for the Muse's wing
Is swift as Cupid's pinion when he flies,
Alarm'd at periwigs and human Tyes).

LIV.

This practice was approv'd in times of yore,

   Though later bards behav'd like gentlemen,

And Garcilasso, Camoens, many more,

   Disclaim'd the privilege of book and pen ;

And bold Aneurin, all bedripp'd with gore,

   Bursting by force from the beleaguer'd glen,

Arrogant, haughty, fierce, of fiery mood,

Not meek and mean, as Gray misunderstood.

LV.

But we, that write a mere Campaigning Tour,

   May choose a station for our point of view

That's picturesque and perfectly secure ;

   Come, now we'll sketch the friar—That will do—

' Designs and etchings by an amateur;'

   ' A frontispiece, and a vignette or two :'

But much I fear that aquatint and etching

Will scarce keep pace with true poetic sketching.

LVI.

Dogs that inhabit near the banks of Nile,

   (As ancient authors or old proverbs say),

Dreading the cruel critic Crocodile,

   Drink as they run, a mouthful and away ;

'Tis a true model for descriptive style ;

   " Keep moving," (as the man says in the play),

The power of motion is the poet's forte—

Therefore, again, " keep moving ! that's your sort !"

LVII.

For, otherwise, while you persist and paint,

   With your portfolio pinion'd to a spot,

Half of your picture grows effac'd and faint,

   Imperfectly remember'd, or forgot ;

Make sketch, then, upon sketch ; and if they a'n't

   Complete, it does not signify a jot ;

Leave graphic illustrations of your work

To be devis'd by Westall or by Smirke.

LVIII.

I'll speak my mind at once, in spite of raillery;

    I've thought and thought again a thousand times,

What a magnificent Poetic Gallery

    Might be design'd from my Stowmarket rhymes;

I look for no reward, nor fee, nor salary,

    I look for England's fame in foreign climes

And future ages—*Honos alit Artes,*

And such a plan would reconcile all parties.

LIX.

I'm strongly for the present state of things;

    I look for no reform, nor innovation,

Because our present Parliaments and Kings

    Are competent to improve and rule the Nation,

Provided Projects that true Genius brings

    Are held in due respect and estimation.

I've said enough—and now you must be wishing

To see the landscape, and the friar fishing.

CANTO IV.

CANTO IV.

_____

I.

A MIGHTY current, unconfin'd and free,

   Ran wheeling round beneath the mountain's shade,

Battering its wave-worn base; but you might see

   On the near margin many a wat'ry glade,

Becalm'd beneath some little island's lee

   All tranquil, and transparent, close embay'd;

Reflecting in the deep serene and even

Each flower and herb, and every cloud of Heaven;

II.

The painted kingfisher, the branch above her,

    Stand in the stedfast mirror fixt and true ;

Anon the fitful breezes brood and hover,

    Fresh'ning the surface with a rougher hue ;

Spreading, withdrawing, pausing, passing over,

    Again returning to retire anew :

So rest and motion, in a narrow range,

Feasted the sight with joyous interchange.

III.

The Monk with handy jerk, and petty baits,

    Stands twitching out apace the perch and roach ;

His mightier tackle, pitch'd apart, awaits

    The groveling barbel's unobserv'd approach:

And soon his motley meal of homely Cates

    Is spread, the leather bottle is a-broach ;

Eggs, Bacon, Ale, a Napkin, Cheese and Knife,

Forming a charming Picture of Still-life.

IV.

The Friar fishing—a design for Cuyp,

A cabinet jewel—' Pray remark the boot;

' And, leading from the light, that shady stripe,

' With the dark bulrush-heads how well they suit;

' And then, that mellow tint so warm and ripe,

' That falls upon the cassock, and surtout :'

If it were fairly painted, puff'd and sold,

My gallery would be worth its weight in gold.

V.

But hark!—the busy Chimes fall fast and strong,

Clattering and pealing in their full career ;

Closely the thickening sounds together throng,

No longer painful to the Friar's ear,

They bind his Fancy with illusion strong;

While his rapt Spirit hears, or seems to hear,

" *Turn, turn again—gen—gèn, thou noble Friar,*

" *Eleele—lèele—lèele—lected Prior.*"

VI.

Thus the mild Monk, as he unhook'd a gudgeon,

    Stood musing—when far other sounds arise,

Sounds of despite and ire, and direful dudgeon ;

    And soon across the River he espies,

In wrathful act, a hideous huge Curmudgeon

    Calling his Comrades on with shouts and cries,

" There !—there it is !—I told them so before ;"

He left his Line and Hook, and said no more ;

VII.

But ran right forward, (pelted all the way),

    And bolted breathless at the Convent-gate,

The messenger and herald of dismay ;

    But soon with conscious worth, and words of weight,

Gives orders which the ready Monks obey :

    Doors, windows, wickets, are blockaded straight ;

He reinspires the Convent's drooping sons,

Is here and there, and every where, at once.

VIII.

" Friends! fellow-Monks!" he cried, (" for well you know

  " That mightiest Giants must in vain essay

" Across yon river's foaming gulf to go :)

  " The mountainous, obscure and winding way,

" That guides their footsteps to the Ford below,

  " Affords a respite of desir'd delay—

" Seize then the passing hour!"—the Monk kept bawling,

In terms to this effect, though not so drawling.

IX.

His words were these, " Before the Ford is crost,

  " We 've a good hour,—at least three quarters good—

" Bestir yourselves, my lads, or all is lost—

  "Drive down this Staunchion, bring those Spars of wood;

" This Bench will serve—here, wedge it to the Post ;

  " Come, Peter, quick! strip off your Gown and Hood—

" Take up the Mallet, Man, and bang away!

" Tighten these Ropes—now lash them, and belay.

X.

" Finish the job while I return—I fear

  " Yon Postern-gate will prove the Convent's ruin ;

" You, brother John, my Namesake! stay you here,

  " And give an eye to what these Monks are doing ;

" Bring out the scalding Sweet-wort, and the Beer,

  " Keep up the Stoke-hole fire, where we were brewing :

" And pull the Gutters up and melt the Lead—

" (Before a dozen aves can be said,)

XI.

" I shall be back amongst you."—Forth he went,

  Secur'd the Postern, and return'd again,

Disposing all with high arbitrement,

  With earnest air, and visage on the main

Concern of public safety fixt and bent;

  For now the Giants, stretching o'er the plain,

Are seen, presenting in the dim horizon

Tall awful forms, horrific and surprising—

XII.

I'd willingly walk barefoot fifty mile,

 To find a scholar, or divine, or squire,

That could assist me to devise a Style

 Fit to describe the conduct of the Friar;

I've tried three different ones within a while,

 The Grave, the Vulgar, and the grand High-flyer;

All are I think improper, more or less,

I'll take my chance amongst 'em—you shall guess.

XIII.

Intrepid, eager, ever prompt to fly

 Where danger and the Convent's safety call;

Where doubtful points demand a judging eye,

 Where on the massy gates huge maces fall;

Where missile vollied rocks are whirl'd on high,

 Pre-eminent upon the embattl'd wall,

In gesture, and in voice, he stands confest;

Exhorting all the Monks to do their best.

XIV.

We redescend to phrase of low degree—

    For there's a point which you must wish to know,

The real ruling Abbot—where was he?

    For (since we make so classical a show,

Our Convent's mighty structure, as you see,

    Like Thebes or Troy beleaguer'd by the foe.

Our Friar scuffling like a kind of Cocles),

You'll figure him perhaps like Eteocles

XV.

In Æschylus, with centries, guards and watches,

    Ready for all contingencies arising,

Pitting his chosen chiefs in equal matches

    Against the foe—anon soliloquizing;

Then occupied anew with fresh dispatches——

    Nothing like this!—but something more surprising—

Was he like Priam then—that's stranger far—

That in the ninth year of his Trojan war,

XVI.

Knew not the names or persons of his foes,

  But merely points them out as stout or tall,

While (as no Trojan knew them, I suppose),

  Helen attends her father to the wall,

To tell him long details of these and those?

  'Twas not like this, but strange and odd withal;

' Nobody knows it—nothing need be said,

' Our poor dear Abbot is this instant dead.

XVII.

' They wheel'd him out, you know, to take the air—

  ' It must have been an apoplectic fit—

' He tumbled forward from his garden-chair—

  ' He seem'd completely gone, but warm as yet:

' I wonder how they came to leave him there;

  ' Poor soul! he wanted courage, heart, and wit

' For Times like these—the Shock and the Surprise!

' 'Twas very natural the Gout should rise.

XVIII.

' But such a sudden end was scarce expected ;

   ' Our parties will be puzzled to proceed ;

' The belfry set divided and dejected :

   ' The crisis is a strange one, strange indeed ;

' I'll bet yon fighting Friar is elected ;

   ' It often happens in the hour of need,

' From popular ideas of utility,

' People are pitch'd upon for mere ability.

XIX.

' I'll hint the subject, and communicate

   ' The sad event—He's standing there apart ;

' Our offer, to be sure, comes somewhat late,

   ' But then, we never thought he meant to start,

' And if he gains his end, at any rate,

   ' He has an understanding and a heart ;

' He'll serve or he'll protect his friends, at least,

' With better spirit than the poor deceas'd ;

XX.

‘ The convent was all going to the devil

   ‘ While he, poor creature, thought himself belov’d

‘ For saying handsome things, and being civil,

   ‘ Wheeling about as he was pull’d and shov’d,

‘ By way of leaving things to find their level.’

   The funeral sermon ended, both approv’d,

And went to Friar John, who merely doubted

The fact, and wish’d them to enquire about it;

XXI.

Then left them, and return’d to the attack :

   They found their Abbot in his former place;

They took him up and turn’d him on his back;

   At first (you know) he tumbled on his face :

They found him fairly stiff, and cold, and black ;

   They *then* unloos’d each ligature and lace,

His neckcloth and his girdle, hose and garters,

And took him up, and lodg’d him in his quarters.

XXII.

Bees serv'd me for a simile before,

 And bees again—' Bees that have lost their king,'
Would seem a repetition and a bore;

 Besides, in fact, I never saw the thing;
And though those phrases from the good old store

 Of " feebler hummings and a flagging wing,"
Perhaps may be descriptive and exact;
I doubt it; I confine myself to fact.

XXIII.

Thus much is certain, that a mighty pother

 Arises; that the frame and the condition
Of things is alter'd, they combine and bother,

 And every winged insect politician
Is warm and eager till they choose another.

 In our monastic Hive the same ambition
Was active and alert; but angry fortune
Constrain'd them to contract the long, importune,

XXIV.

Tedious, obscure, inexplicable train,

   Qualification, form, and oath and test,

Ballots on ballots, ballotted again ;

   Accessits, scrutinies, and all the rest ;

Theirs was the good old method, short and plain ,

   Per acclamationem they invest

Their fighting Friar John with Robes and Ring,

Crozier and Mitre, Seals, and every thing.

XXV.

With a new warlike active Chief elected,

   Almost at once, it scarce can be conceiv'd

What a new spirit, real or affected,

   Prevail'd throughout; the monks complain'd and griev'd

That nothing was attempted or projected ;

   While Quiristers and Novices believ'd

That their new fighting Abbot, Friar John,

Would sally forth at once, and lead them on.

XXVI.

I pass such gossip, and devote my cares
    By diligent enquiry to detect
The genuine state and posture of affairs :
    Unmanner'd, uninform'd, and incorrect,
Falsehood and Malice hold alternate chairs,
    And lecture and preside in Envy's sect ;
The fortunate and great she never spares,
Sowing the soil of history with tares.

XXVII.

Thus, jealous of the truth, and feeling loth
    That Sir Nathaniel henceforth should accuse
Our noble Monk of cowardice and sloth,
    I'll print the Affidavit of the Muse,
And state the facts as ascertain'd on Oath,
    Corroborated by Surveys and Views,
When good King Arthur granted them a Brief,
And Ninety Groats were rais'd for their relief.

XXVIII.

Their arbours, walks, and alleys were defac'd,
    Riven and uprooted, and with ruin strown,
And the fair Dial in their garden plac'd
    Batter'd by barbarous hands, and overthrown;
The Deer with wild pursuit dispers'd and chas'd,
    The Dove-house ransack'd, and the Pigeons flown;
The Cows all kill'd in one promiscuous slaughter,
The Sheep all drown'd, and floating in the water.

XXIX.

The Mill was burn'd down to the water wheels;
    The Giants broke away the Dam and Sluice,
Dragg'd up and emptied all the Fishing-reels;
    Drain'd and destroy'd the Reservoir and Stews,
Wading about, and groping carp and eels;
    In short, no single earthly thing of use
Remain'd untouch'd beyond the convent's wall:
The Friars from their windows view'd it all.

XXX.

But the bare hope of personal defence,
    The church, the convent's, and their own protection,
Absorb'd their thoughts, and silenc'd every ser e
  `Of present loss, till Friar John's election;
Then other schemes arose, I know not whence,
    Whether from flattery, zeal, or disaffection,
But the brave Monk, like Fabius with Hannibal,
Against internal faction, and the cannibal

XXXI.

Inhuman foe, that threaten'd from without,
    Stood firmly, with a self-sufficing mind,
Impregnable to rumour, fear, or doubt,
    Determin'd that the casual, idle, blind
Event of battle with that barbarous Rout,
    Flush'd with success and garbage, should not bind
Their future destinies, or fix the seal
Of ruin on the claustral Common-weal.

XXXII.

He check'd the rash, the boisterous, and the proud,
 By speech and action, manly but discreet;
During the siege he never once allow'd
 Of chapters, or convok'd the monks to meet,
Dreading the consultations of a crowd.
 Historic parallels we sometimes meet—
I think I could contrive one—if you please,
I shall compare our Monk to Pericles.

XXXIII.

In Former Times, amongst the Athenians bold,
 This Pericles was plac'd in high command,
Heading their troops (as statesmen us'd of old),
 In all their wars and fights by sea and land;
Besides, in Langhorne's Plutarch we are told
 How many fine ingenious things he plann'd;
For Phidias was an Architect and Builder,
Jeweller and Engraver, Carver, Gilder;

E

XXXIV.

But altogether quite expert and clever;

    Pericles took him up and stood his friend,

Persuading these Athenians to endeavour

    To raise a Work to last to the world's end,

By means of which their Fame should last for ever;

    Likewise an Image (which, you comprehend,

They meant to pray to, for the country's good):

They had before an old one made of wood,

XXXV.

But being partly rotten and decay'd,

    They wish'd to have a new one spick and span,

So Pericles advis'd it should be made

    According to this Phidias's plan,

Of ivory, with gold all overlaid,

    Of the height of twenty cubits and a span,

Making eleven yards of English measure,

All to be paid for from the public treasure.

XXXVI.

So Phidias's talents were requited

With talents that were spent upon the work,

And every body busied and delighted,

Building a Temple—this was their next quirk—

Lest it should think itself ill-used and slighted.

This Temple now belongs to the Grand Turk,

The finest in the world allowed to be,

That people go five hundred miles to see.

XXXVII.

Its ancient Carvings are safe here at home,

Brought round by shipping from as far as Greece,

Finer, they say, than all the things at Rome;

But here you need not pay a penny-piece;

But curious people, if they like to come,

May look at them as often as they please—

I've left my subject, but I was not sorry

To mention things that raise the country's glory

E 2

XXXVIII.

Well, Pericles made every thing complete,

　　Their town, their harbour, and their city wall;

When their allies rebell'd, he made them treat

　　And pay for peace, and tax'd and fin'd them all,

By which means Pericles maintain'd a fleet,

　　And kept three hundred gallies at his call;

Pericles was a man for every thing;

Pericles was a kind of petty king.

XXXIX.

It happen'd Sparta was another State;

　　They thought themselves as good; they could not bear

To see the Athenians grown so proud and great,

　　Ruling and domineering every where,

And so resolv'd, before it grew too late,

　　To fight it out and settle the affair;

Then, being quite determin'd to proceed,

They muster'd an amazing force indeed;

XL.

And (after praying to their idol Mars)

    March'd on, with all the allies that chose to join,

As was the practice in old heathen wars,

    Destroying all the fruit trees, every vine,

And smashing and demolishing the jars

    In which those classic ancients kept their wine;

The Athenians ran within the city wall

To save themselves, their children, wives, and all.

XLI.

Then Pericles (whom they compar'd to Jove,

    As being apt to storm and play the deuce),

Kept quiet, and forbad the troops to move,

    Because a battle was no kind of use;

The more they mutinied, the more he strove

    To keep them safe in spite of their abuse,

For while the Farms were ransack'd round the Town,

This was the people's language up and down:

XLII.

' 'Tis better to die once than live to see

   ' Such an abomination, such a waste ;'

' No! no !' says Pericles, ' that must not be,

   ' You're too much in hurry,—too much haste—

' Learned Athenians, leave the thing to me ;

   ' You think of being bullied and disgrac'd ;

' Don't think of that, nor answer their defiance;

' We'll gain the day by our superior science.'

XLIII.

Pericles led the people as he pleas'd,

   But in most cases something is forgot :

What with the crowd and heat they grew diseas'd,

   And died in heaps like wethers with the rot ;

And, at the last, the same distemper seiz'd

   Poo᷍ Pericles himself—he went to pot.

It answer'd badly:—therefore I admire

So much the more the conduct of the Friar.

XLIV.

For in the Garrison where he presided,

   Neither distress, nor famine, nor disease,

Were felt, nor accident nor harm betided

   The happy Monks; but plenteous, and with ease,

All needful monkish viands were provided;

   Bacon and Pickled-herring, Pork and Peas;

And when the Table-beer began to fail,

They found resources in the Bottled-ale.

XLV.

Dinner and supper kept their usual hours;

   Breakfast and luncheon never were delay'd,

While to the Centries on the walls and towers

   Between two plates hot messes were convey'd.

At the departure of the invading powers,

   It was a boast the noble Abbot made,

None of his Monks were weaker, paler, thinner,

Or, during all the siege, had lost a dinner.

XLVI.

This was the common course of their hostility;

    The giant forces being foil'd at first,

Had felt the manifest impossibility

    Of carrying things before them at a burst,

But still, without a prospect of utility,

    At stated hours they pelted, howl'd, and curs'd;

And sometimes, at the peril of their pates,

Would bang with clubs and maces at the gates;

XLVII.

Them the brave monkish legions, unappall'd,

    With stones that serv'd before to pave the court,

(Heap'd and prepar'd at hand), repell'd and maul'd,

    Without an effort, smiling as in sport,

With many a broken head, and many a scald

    From stones and molten lead and boiling wort;

Thus little Pillicock was left for dead,

And old Loblolly forc'd to keep his bed.

XLVIII.

The giant-troops invariably withdrew,

   (Like mobs in Naples, Portugal, and Spain),

To dine at twelve o'clock, and sleep till two,

   And afterwards (except in case of rain),

Return'd to clamour, hoot, and pelt anew.

   The scene was every day the same again;

Thus the Blockade grew tedious : I intended

A week ago, myself, to raise and end it.

XLIX.

One morn the drowsy Centry rubb'd his eyes,

   Foil'd by the scanty, baffling, early light ;

It seem'd, a Figure of inferior size

   Was traversing the Giants' camp outright ;

And soon a Monkish Form they recognize—

   And now their brother Martin stands in sight,

That on that morning of alarm and fear

Had rambled out to see the Salmon-Weir ;

L.

Passing the Ford, the Giants' first attack

   Left brother Martin's station in their rear,

And thus prevented him from falling back;

   But during all the Siege he watch'd them near,

Saw them returning by their former Track

   The Night before, and found the Camp was clear;

And so return'd in safety with delight

And rapture, and a ravenous appetite.

LI.

" Well! welcome,—welcome, brother!—Brother Martin!

   " Why, Martin!—we could scarce believe our eyes:

" Ah, brother! strange events here since our parting—"

   And Martin din'd (dispensing brief replies

To all the questions that the monks were starting,

   Betwixt his mouthfuls), while each friar vies

In filling, helping, carving, questioning;

So Martin din'd in public like a king.

LII.

And now the Gates are open'd, and the Throng

    Forth issuing, the deserted Camp survey;

' Here Murdomack, and Mangonel the strong,

    ' And Gorboduc were lodg'd,' and ' here,' they say,

' This pigsty to Poldavy did belong;

    ' Here Brindleback, and here Phagander lay.'

They view the deep indentures, broad and round,

Which mark their posture squatting on the ground.

LIII.

Then to the traces of gigantic feet,

    Huge, wide apart, with half a dozen toes;

They track them on, till they converge and meet,

    (An earnest and assurance of repose)

Close at the Ford; the cause of this retreat

    They all conjecture, but no creature knows;

It was ascrib'd to causes multifarious,

To saints, as Jerom, George and Januarius,

LIV.

To their own pious founder's intercession,

    To Ave-Maries, and our Lady's Psalter;

To news that Friar John was in possession,

    To new wax candles plac'd upon the altar,

To their own prudence, valour, and discretion;

    To reliques, rosaries, and holy water ;

To beads and psalms, and feats of arms—in short,

There was no end of their accounting for't.

LV.

But though they could not, you, perhaps, may guess;

    They went, in short, upon their last adventure :

After the Ladies—neither more nor less—

    Our story now revolves upon its centre,

And I'm rejoic'd myself, I must confess,

    To find it tally like an old indenture;

They drove off Mules and Horses half a score,

The same that you saw roasted heretofore.

LVI.

Our Giants' memoirs still remain on hand,

   For all my notions, being genuine gold,

Beat out beneath the hammer and expand,

   And multiply themselves a thousand fold

Beyond the first idea that I plann'd;

   Besides,—this present copy must be sold:

Besides,—I promis'd Murray t'other day,

To let him have it by the tenth of May.

END OF CANTO IV.

T. DAVISON, LOMBARD-STREET, WHITEFRIARS, LONDON.